THE CHINESE HOROSCOPES LIBRARY

ROOSTER

KWOK MAN-HO

A DORLING KINDERSLEY BOOK

Senior Editor — Sharon Lucas
Art Editor — Camilla Fox
Managing Editor — Krystyna Mayer
Managing Art Editor — Derek Coombes
DTP Designer — Doug Miller
Production Controller — Antony Heller
US Editor — Laaren Brown

Artworks: Danuta Mayer 4, 8, 11, 17, 27, 29, 31, 33, 35;
Giuliano Fornari 21; Jane Thomson; Sarah Ponder.

Special Photography by Steve Gorton. Thank you to the Bristol City Museum & Art Gallery, Oriental Section; The British Museum, Chinese Post Office, Percival David Foundation of Chinese Art, and The Powell-Cotton Museum.

Additional Photography: Eric Crichton, Mike Dunning, Jo Foord, Philip Gatward, Steve Gorton, Liz McAulay, Stephen Oliver, Tim Ridley, Karl Shone, Clive Streeter.

Picture Credits: Bridgeman Art Library/Oriental Museum, Durham University 19bl; Bruce Coleman/Gerald Cubitt 20bl.

First American Edition, 1994
4 6 8 10 9 7 5

Published in the United States by DK Publishing, Inc., 95 Madison Avenue,
New York, New York 10016

ISBN 1-56458-609-X
Library of Congress Catalog Number 93-48006

Reproduced by GRB Editrice, Verona, Italy
Printed and bound in Hong Kong by Imago

CONTENTS

INTRODUCING CHINESE HOROSCOPES

For thousands of years, the Chinese have used their astrology and religion to establish a harmony between people and the world around them.

The exact origins of the twelve animals of Chinese astrology – the Rat, Ox, Tiger, Rabbit, Dragon, Snake, Horse, Ram, Monkey, Rooster, Dog, and Pig – remain a mystery. Nevertheless, these animals are important in Chinese astrology. They are much more than general signposts to the year and to the possible good or bad times ahead for us all. The twelve animals of Chinese astrology are considered to be a reflection of the Universe itself.

YIN AND YANG

The many differences in our natures, moods, health, and fortunes reflect the wider changes within the Universe. The Chinese believe that

YIN AND YANG SYMBOL
White represents the female force of yin, and black represents the masculine force of yang.

every single thing in the Universe is held in balance by the dynamic, cosmic forces of yin and yang. Yin is feminine, watery, and cool; the force of the Moon and the rain. Yang is masculine, solid, and hot; the force of the Sun and the Earth. According to ancient Chinese belief, the concentrated essences of yin and yang became the four seasons, and the scattered essences of yin and yang became the myriad creatures that are found on Earth.

The twelve animals of Chinese astrology are all associated with either yin or yang. The forces of yin rise as Winter approaches. These forces decline with the warmth of Spring, when yang begins to assert elf. Even in the course of a normal y, yin and yang are at work, nstantly changing and balancing. ese forces also naturally rise and l within us all.

Everyone has their own internal lance of yin and yang. This affects r tempers, ambitions, and health. e also respond to the changes of eather, to the environment, and to e people who surround us.

HE FIVE ELEMENTS
l that we can touch, taste, or see is vided into five basic types or ements – wood, fire, earth, gold, d water. Everything in the niverse can be linked to one of ese elements.

For example, the element gold is ked to the Monkey and to the ooster. This element is also linked the color white, acrid-tasting od, the season of Autumn, and the

emotion of sorrow. The activity of these elements indicates the fortune that may befall us.

AN INDIVIDUAL DISCOVERY
Chinese astrology can help you balance your yin and yang. It can also tell you which element you are, and the colors, tastes, parts of the body, or emotions that are linked to your particular sign. Your fortune can be prophesied according to the year, month, day, and hour in which you were born. You can identify the type of people to whom you are attracted, and the career that will suit your character. You can understand your changes of mood, your reactions to other places and to other people. In essence, you can start to discover what makes you an individual.

DIVINATION STICKS
Another ancient and popular method of Chinese fortune-telling is using special divination sticks to obtain a specific reading from prediction books.

CASTING YOUR HOROSCOPE

The Chinese calendar is based on the movement of the Moon, unlike the calendar used in the Western world, which is based on the movement of the Sun.

Before you begin to cast your Chinese horoscope, check your year of birth on the chart on pages 44 to 45. Check particularly carefully if you were born in the early months of the year. The Chinese year does not usually begin until January or February, and you might belong to the previous Chinese year. For example, if you were born in 1961 you might assume that you were born in the Year of the Ox. However, if your birthday falls before February 15 you belong to the previous Chinese year, which is the Year of the Rat.

THE SIXTY-YEAR CYCLE

The Chinese measure the passing of time by cycles of sixty years. The twelve astrological animals appear five times during the sixty-year cycle, and they appear in a slightly different form every time. For example, if you were born in 1969

you are a Rooster Announcing the Dawn, but if you were born in 198 you are a Rooster in the Cage.

MONTHS, DAYS, AND HOURS

The twelve lunar months of the Chinese calendar do not correspond exactly with the twelve Western calendar months. This is because Chinese months are lunar, whereas Western months are solar. Chinese months are normally twenty-nine t thirty days long, and every three to four years an extra month is added keep approximately in step with th Western year.

One Chinese hour is equal to tw Western hours, and the twelve Chinese hours correspond to the twelve animal signs.

The year, month, day, and hour of birth are the keys to Chinese astrology. Once you know them, you can start to unlock your person Chinese horoscope.

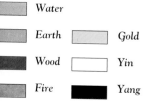

Water

Earth

Wood

Fire

Gold

Yin

Yang

CHINESE ASTROLOGICAL WHEEL

In the center of the wheel is the yin and yang symbol. It is surrounded by the Chinese astrological character linked to each animal. The band of color indicates your element, and the outer ring reveals whether you are yin or yang.

· ROOSTER ·
MYTHS AND LEGENDS

The Jade Emperor, heaven's ruler, asked to see the Earth's twelve
most interesting animals. When they arrived, he was impressed
by the Rooster's eloquence, and awarded it tenth place.

In China, the Rooster is believed to ward off evil. A picture of a red rooster is hung up to protect the house from fire, while a white rooster placed on a coffin is reputed to keep demons at bay. The Rooster also symbolizes courage and male vigor. It is not eaten in China, but there is a tradition of rooster fighting that continues today, even though it is strictly prohibited. A crowing rooster symbolizes great achievement, and a gift of a rooster with a fine comb expresses the wish that the recipient will be granted an official post.

ROOSTER DISH WITH PEONIES
This ancient Chinese dish depicts a
rooster, a butterfly, and peonies, which
symbolize wealth and distinction.

THE ROOSTER AND HIS COMB

Long ago there was a hunter who hunted by day and tended his lovely garden in the evenings. One day he found his favorite mulberry bush shriveled and wilting. He did all he could to save it, but it perished. The hunter shouted to the sun, "You are too hot and have destroyed my pretty bush. I am going to get my revenge."

Taking aim with his bow and arrow, the hunter fired at the sun, and the arrow hit the sun straight in the eye. The sun cried out in pain and ran to hide self behind the clouds. All the animals of the kingdom urged the sun to come out again, but it stayed behind the clouds. Soon the land grew extremely dark and cold, and the animals realized that they would die if the sun did not appear. They called a great council and decided to try their best to persuade the sun to come out again.

The first to volunteer to call the sun was the Ox, but his voice was so deep and low that the sun could not hear it. The Tiger was next, but his roared message sounded so fierce and terrifying that the sun hid even deeper into the clouds.

At last the Rooster strutted into the Council. "Let me try," he said, somewhat arrogantly, and called out loud and clear. The sun heard the rooster's agreeable voice and peered out. The rooster called again, reassuringly, and the sun came out completely and told the rooster, "I will give you a very special comb to comb your feathers before you call me each morning."

The sun threw down the comb and the rooster ran to catch it. Unfortunately, in his excitement, the rooster mistimed the catch, and the comb landed upside down on his head, where it remains to this day.

HAN DYNASTY HEADS
These bronze rooster heads are finials and date from China's Han dynasty.

13

· ROOSTER ·
PERSONALITY

The Rooster has an open and courageous nature, and will always make itself available for others in need. It enjoys, and openly indulges in, the good things in life.

You are excellent company, and usually adapt well to different circumstances. Maintaining your appearance takes up a considerable amount of your time, and you are just as critical about your own taste as you are about others'.

MOTIVATION

You enjoy the best of everything and want your needs to be met. You expect to follow your own routine without any interference from other people.

However, there is a certain innocence in your approach, and your selfishness is never intended to

ROOSTERS AND FLOWERS
This Chinese porcelain vessel is decorated with exquisitely painted roosters and flowers.

be hurtful. Although you are often straightforward to the point of shamelessness, this is not through vindictiveness, but because you feel that others should know the truth.

THE INNER ROOSTER

Superficially, you are charming and rarely exhibit the true depth of your extensive knowledge. In reality, you have an independent spirit and are wary of others. Although you possess a streak of exhibitionism, you also have a compassionate side. This altruism tends to come to the fore when others ask for your help.

ou are trustworthy and offer
nsible advice, but you rarely reveal
urself to other people and may
metimes appear to be rather off-
nd and erratic.

You have a vulnerable nature and
ten feel insecure, but you hide
ese weaknesses beneath humor and
nversation. Your true nature is
ually seen only by your close
ends or in times of crisis.

You are a sociable and
arming romantic partner. It is
fficult for you to commit
urself, but once you have, you
e dependable and responsible.

As a parent, you are dedicated
d organized. You can also be
ry protective, but always like to
ve yourself the freedom to
joy life's luxuries.

HE ROOSTER CHILD

e young Rooster is open,
quisitive, and good company, but
interests may have to be subtly
rected by its parents.

ANDING ROOSTER

*e jaunty stance of this standing
oster suggests the natural pride
d self-confidence of the Rooster
rsonality. The figure is porcelain
d is from 18th-century China.*

· ROOSTER ·
LOVE

The Rooster is a charming creature. It loves fine clothes and good company, and always wants to impress. Usually, it has a trail of besotted admirers.

You relish an element of conquest in love. Romance must never be easy and predictable for you – if it is, you are soon likely to be off in search of the excitement of a new partner.

Your independence is vital, and life could be difficult for a partner who needs you to be by his or her side. You are jealous, but are careful not to show it.

Once you feel that you are truly involved in an emotional relationship, you make an intelligent and agreeable partner. In the security of a committed relationship, you are willing to allow your sensitivities and vulnerabilities to surface.

You are renowned for your honesty, but can sometimes appear to be brutally offhand. Unintentionally, this behavior could hurt the one you love.

Ideally, you are suited to the Ox and the Snake. The Ox can offer sociability, excitement and the security that you secretly need. The Snake shares your love of clothes and color, but also appreciates your more subtle side.

GODDESS OF LOVE
Kuan Yin is a powerful figure in Chinese mytholo. Once a male Buddhist de she is now known as th goddess of mercy, and as Sung-tzu, the giver of children.

d your animal sign, then look for
 animals that share its
 ckground color – the Rooster
 s a yellow background and
 most compatible with the
 x and the Snake. The
 mbol in the center of
 wheel represents
 uble happiness.

 e Dragon welcomes
 ur attention and
 ares your love of
 rformance. The Pig
 ould be tolerant and
 derstanding, and will
 nore your boastfulness or
iticisms. The Rat may prove to be
 lifficult partner unless you allow it
 see beneath your surface.

The Tiger and the Rabbit could
 ove too critical – you may push the
 abbit's patience to the limit, and
 the Tiger may judge

ORCHID
In China, the
orchid, or Lan
Hua, is an emblem
of love and beauty. It is
also a fertility symbol
and represents
many offspring.

you too quickly. A relationship with
the Horse could prove to be very
competitive, and although you can
provide the Ram with comfort and
security, it is likely to be too
unconventional for you. Your
honesty complements the Monkey's
astuteness and audacity, but it could
take some time to understand and
trust each other.

Although a partnership with
another Rooster would undoubtedly
be lively, it is also likely to be full
of turbulence and disagreement.

· ROOSTER ·
CAREER

The Rooster is intuitive, intelligent, and well organized. It does not enjoy being told what to do and is best suited to careers with an element of independence.

TAILOR
The work of the tailor requires a combination of practical skill and creative flair. This suits the Rooster well, since it is confident, convincing, and capable, and has an eye for clothes and color.

Sewing machine

FASHION DESIGNER
Style is of great interest to the extravagant Rooster. It loves to create anything new and different, and could derive great satisfaction from a career as a fashion designer.

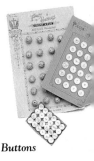

Patterns

Buttons

ENTERTAINER

The Rooster is a natural entertainer. It is relaxing company and enjoys socializing, whatever the occasion. When entertaining, the Rooster enjoys using beautiful objects, such as this Chinese chocolate pot from the late K'ang-hsi or Yung Chen reign (c.1720–1735) and early 17th-century Ming dynasty tea bowl.

Chinese chocolate pot

Chinese tea bowl

SERVICE WORKER

A career as a service worker suits the Rooster, because it is never afraid to accept challenges and is rarely defeated by obstacles. It always needs to retain some independence, however.

Railroad worker's whistle

Firefighter's helmet

BEAUTICIAN

The beautician's work appeals to the Rooster's flamboyance. It would adore this 19th-century Chinese silver fingernail protector.

Beautician's bottle

Fingernail protector

HEALTH

Yin and yang are in a continual state of flux within the body. Good health is dependent upon the balance of yin and yang being constantly harmonious.

There is a natural minimum and maximum level of yin and yang in the human body. The body's energy is known as ch'i and is a yang force. The movement of ch'i in the human body is complemented by the movement of blood, which is a yin force. The very slightest displacement of the fine balance of yin or yang in the human body can quickly lead to poor health and sickness. However,

LINGCHIH FUNGUS
The fungus shown in this detail from a Ch'ing dynasty bowl is the "immortal" lingchih fungus, which symbolizes longevity.

LOTUS FLOWER
The seeds of the lotus flower are rich in vitamin C and are combined with lily to restore ch'i.

yang illness can be cured by yin treatment, and yin illness can be cured by yang treatment. Everybody has their own individual balance of yin and yang. It is likely that a hot-tempered person will have strong yang forces, and that a peaceful person will have strong yin forces. Your nature is closely identified with your health, and before Chinese medicine can be prescribed, your moods must be carefully taken into account. A balance of joy, anger, sadness, happiness, worry, pensiveness, and fear must always be maintained. The fine balance is known in China as the Harmony of the Seven Sentiments.

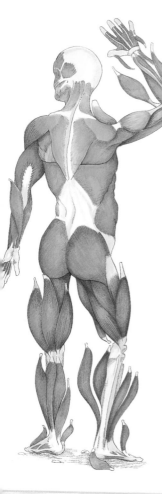

Born in the Year of the Rooster, you are associated with the element gold. This element is linked with the lungs, large intestine, nose, skin, and hair. These are the parts of the human body that are most relevant to the pattern of your health. You are also associated with the emotion of sorrow and with acrid-tasting food.

The lotus flower (*Nelumbo nucifera*) is associated with your astrological sign. Its seeds are used to strengthen the spleen and stomach, promote mental stability, and control the loss of body fluids.

In China, lotus seed and lily soup is served at the end of wedding banquets. This is because their Chinese names form a pun on "continuous sons" and "one hundred together," and the soup represents a wish for one hundred years of married life, with many sons.

Chinese medicine is specific; therefore, never take lotus seeds or any other herb unless you are following advice from a doctor.

ASTROLOGY AND ANATOMY

Your element, gold, is associated with two major organs, the lungs and the large intestine. The lungs are yin, and the large intestine is yang.

· ROOSTER ·
LEISURE

The Rooster is a natural performer and loves being the center of attention. However, it also likes to escape to a private, comfortable place where it can truly relax.

EXERCISING

Morning exercise is particularly beneficial for the Rooster, because it helps it prepare for the energetic day ahead. Jumping a rope and running appeal to the Rooster, because they are forms of exercise that can be done at virtually any time.

Jump rope

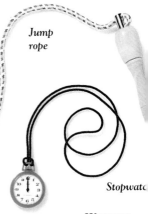

Stopwatc

Exercise shoes

WALKING

Although walking ma seem to be too tame f the highly sociable Rooster, it is a valuab pastime. Walking provides the Rooster w a relaxing escape from usual frenetic activity

HOME ACCOUNTING

The Rooster is extravagant with its money. Luckily, it is very well organized, and always keeps a careful eye on its spending habits.

Home accounts book and calculator

Alto saxophone

ROOSTER LOGO

The French brothers Charles and Emile Pathé set up a film company, which produced newsreels after 1909. This rooster is their company's distinctive logo.

Microphone

Pathé Brothers' logo

PERFORMING

The limelight is the Rooster's natural environment. It is a flamboyant perfomer, whatever the occasion or the company. It would thrive on the exposure provided by a solo saxophone performance or by singing to a large cabaret audience.

SYMBOLISM

*Each astrological animal is linked with a certain food,
direction, color, emotion, association, and symbol. The
Rooster is also associated with the season of Autumn.*

**Chinese
porcelain
rooster**

COLOR

*In China, brilliant white is
the color of purity. It is also
the color that is linked with
the Rooster. This porcelain
blanc de chine Rooster is from
China's Ch'ing dynasty.*

Cloves

FOOD

*Acrid foods, such as cloves, are
associated with the Rooster.*

24

T-square

Antique Chinese compass

SYMBOL
The Rooster's symbol in Chinese astrology is the T-square.

DIRECTION
The Chinese compass points south, whereas the Western compass points north. The Rooster's direction is the west.

EMOTION
Sorrow is the emotion that is connected with the Rooster.

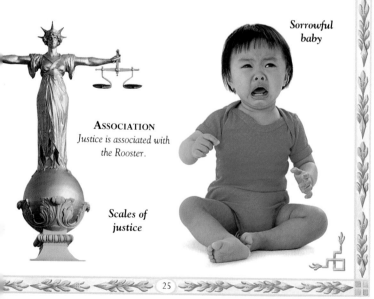

ASSOCIATION
Justice is associated with the Rooster.

Scales of justice

Sorrowful baby

SINGING ROOSTER

~ 1945 2005 ~

*In Chinese mythology, the Rooster is considered to be a very
courageous creature. As a result, it is often carved on the
tops of houses as a protection against evil spirits.*

As the Singing Rooster, you are
associated with success and
expansion. Perhaps this is similar to
the chest of a confident Rooster,
which swells when the Rooster is
singing or feels proud.

PERSONALITY
You tend to be extremely outspoken
and fearless, and your powers of
articulation are immense. It is likely
to be your sincere belief that you
should talk about everything that you
see and hear.

You invariably feel that what you
consider to be wrong should be
denounced, and that in the same
way, what you consider to be right
should be praised.

Although this honesty is very
admirable, it is unlikely to make you
many friends, at least not at first.
Because you set yourself high
standards and are always more than

willing to speak out and make your
views known, you tend to expect
other people to do the same as a
matter of course.

This natural idealism makes it
very hard for you to suffer fools
gladly. Perhaps you should try a bit
harder, for a little tolerance may
make life considerably more
pleasurable for you, as well as for
those around you.

CAREER
Luckily, your forthright manner do
not hinder any success in your
career. You should find that life
treats you well, and if you are
sensible with money, you will tend
to prosper.

FRIENDSHIPS
You are linked with blossoming. Th
is auspicious, for it represents
longevity. Since Singing Roosters

Singing Rooster

njoy long life, it is even more
mportant for you to try and control
our tendency to offend people –
ou may need your friends for many
ears to come.

FAMILY

our family has immense importance
n your life. You will probably have a
good relationship with your parents
nd should be able to get along well
ith your siblings, even though they
nay be in awe of you.

The essential value of a contented
amily life is fully appreciated by
ou, and you are always likely to do
everything in your power to ensure
that your family remains happy,
peaceful, and stable.

Beware, however, of expecting
too much from your children. Be
generous, and try to give them the
freedom to be themselves.

RELATIONSHIPS

You may be slightly wild in your
emotional affairs before you commit
yourself. However, once you have
found your partner you are likely to
become family oriented. Your
partner and your children should find
you a supportive companion.

27

LONELY ROOSTER

~ 1957 2017 ~

This Rooster stands apart from the bustle of the farmyard. It is not a sad creature, however. Though it sometimes finds life a struggle, the Lonely Rooster is very caring.

You are associated with a bee sting. Symbolically, this suggests that just as the bee that stings must suffer death, so you must suffer some loneliness while you pursue your sense of identity.

YOUTH

At school, you may have found it difficult to be part of a crowd. In the same way, during your early years at work, you invariably found the cut and thrust of a working life difficult to cope with. Most dynamic environments are likely to disturb you in your youth, because they are alien to your personality.

PERSONALITY

You have a caring and gentle personality and are upset by aggressive behavior. You need to be well liked, and you also enjoy making other people happy.

Ironically, this desire to make everyone feel comfortable can put you at a disadvantage. This should change when you have greater control over situations, however.

You can be particularly liberal with your cash and also with your credit. This generosity comes naturally to you but can sometimes turn into a hindrance, for bad debts may have a detrimental affect on your good friendships.

FRIENDSHIPS

Try to distinguish between the occasions when people are actually need of your financial help and the times when they require your spiritual or moral support.

Unfortunately, the unscrupulou might sometimes consider you to b very easily parted from your money Perhaps it will prove most beneficia for you to remember that having a

Lonely Rooster

ntle and caring nature is not
cessarily to be equated with being
ly and sentimental.

ROSPECTS
s you grow older, people in
fluential positions should find that
u are exactly the type of person
ey want to work with and to have
a friend. This is likely to bring you
any rewards.

Your prospects should be furthered,
for you will be operating in a mature
social circle. Here, you are likely to
be fully appreciated for the person
you are and for the way in which you
treat others.

Hopefully, you should find that
the difficulties of your youth will be
more than compensated for by the
considerable advantages of middle
age and beyond.

ROOSTER ANNOUNCING THE DAWN

~ 1909 1969 ~

This is the Rooster in its natural position — loudly heralding the glorious new day. It will announce the dawn whether or not anyone wishes to hear its song.

You are associated with a cutting instrument — something that does an efficient job, but that may also scythe things down.

PERSONALITY

You tend to say and do what you think is right, without worrying about the consequences. You are prone to go charging in when caution might dictate otherwise.

Unfortunately, your behavior sometimes upsets and disturbs people, but you feel that it is your duty to behave in this way.

However, you are very clever. Perhaps you should hold on to your sense of doing what is right but also fuse it with your wisdom.

Once you allow yourself to admit it, you are, in fact, a very considerate person indeed. Try to allow this side of your personality to have more

dominance. As a result, people should listen more carefully to whatever you have to say.

FAMILY

You are likely to have your children rather late in life. This is probably for the best, since your maturity should make you value your children all the more.

It may take you many years to learn how to cope with the more difficult aspects of your personality. Consequently, you may find that you have estranged yourself from your parents and siblings.

Always be prepared to rebuild the bridges between you. Your parents and your siblings probably had to endure considerable aggravation from you in the past; therefore it is only fair for you to make an effort in your newly found maturity.

Rooster Announcing the Dawn

ELATIONSHIPS

might take some time to find the
ght partner, but you should have a
ppy committed relationship.

ROSPECTS

ou should enjoy a successful life and
prosperous career. Take care with
oney, for you possess two
nflicting trends within your
rsonality. You have the capacity to
be very careful with your money, or
even stingy, but you are also capable
of suddenly deciding that you want
to waste your money on the most
unnecessary fripperies.

Make every effort to control this
duality, for it could complicate your
life. Enjoy your money by all means,
but do not allow your extreme love
of spending to deteriorate into
uncontrolled binging.

ROOSTER IN THE CAGE

~ 1921 1981 ~

There are two powerful strands within this Rooster, which must be kept in harmony. It is associated with two hands that are trying to balance something.

This Rooster is likely to be well cared for and well fed. It may even be treated as a pet and should lead a very easy life.

Such a pampered lifestyle does have its disadvantages, however, for this Rooster may find that it is being fattened up for a future meal. Even if there are no immediate plans to eat this Rooster, its freedom to roam and forage is likely to be limited.

PERSONALITY

Essentially, there are two sides to your personality. Everything in life may seem to be going your way – you are likely to be successful and to get what you want. People probably pay you lots of attention, and you are very clever. You are enjoyable company and tend to be a natural performer. You like to show yourself off and dress well, and you tend to be able to hold your own in any argument. Other people often find your skills and your knowledge highly impressive.

FAMILY

This is only half of your life story, however. The other half is that you may experience severe difficulties with your family. You may have disappointed them, and they could have problems in getting along with you. In this delicate family situation you are most likely to resemble a cooped-up, frustrated Rooster.

RELATIONSHIPS

You may experience similar difficulties in your committed relationship. Perhaps your partner does not always respond to you with the enthusiasm or admiration that you might like. Bear in mind that this might be because you are being rather arrogant, even "cocky."

Rooster in the Cage

Although you are undoubtedly clever and highly accomplished, this does not necessarily mean that people have to lavish you with constant praise. It might be valuable for you to learn a little humility.

Once you have your arrogance under some sort of control, you should find that your life, successful as it is, will become even more enjoyable and fulfilling.

PROSPECTS

Throughout your life, you are often likely to experience a sense of being restricted or of not being as fully appreciated as you might expect. Perhaps your expectations are too unrealistic. Try not to expect too much from other people, and concentrate instead on the undeniable friendships and the many achievements that you have made.

ROOSTER IN THE HEN ROOST

~ 1933 1993 ~

This could be seen as the ultimate location for the Rooster:
in the hen roost, it should be fully appreciated.
Consequently, this is an auspicious sign.

You are associated with doing what is right and being able to enjoy the resulting good fortune.

PERSONALITY

You have a lively, vivacious personality. Even though you may always seem to be on the verge of trouble, somehow you manage to land on your feet. You may sometimes seem a little wild, but no one should mind your behavior too much. You are frank, open, and likable. However, you have a tendency to gossip, which could alienate some people. You are fortunate and tend to retain your friendships, even when you may have revealed a confidence.

CAREER

Progress in your career may not go smoothly, but you are never likely to find yourself in serious trouble. In a business partnership, you are likely to be absolutely convinced that you will do well. Unfortunately, your business partners might not share your confidence. Try to learn to operate at their pace; otherwise, you might find their apparent slowness highly irritating.

FAMILY

Your family background may seem to be against your business interests, but as usual, you should be able to make a success of your situation. This might cause some resentment, but you are advised to be generous in your response.

RELATIONSHIPS

Your committed relationship is likely to be happy, even though the thoughtlessness of your actions could sometimes put it under great strain. Try to be more considerate, and do

Rooster in the Hen Roost

...ot always rely on your innate good ...rtune to see you through. Any sign ...f thoughtfulness or consideration ...om you is likely to ensure a happier ...ommitted relationship.

PROSPECTS

...t is highly unlikely that you will ever ...nd yourself short of financial ...esources. Although you always tend ...o spend much more lavishly than ...ou should, good luck invariably ...omes to the rescue.

...You should try to take care, ...owever, for a sense of ...verconfidence could lead to disaster. You are a naturally fortunate person, but do not be tempted to push your luck too far.

The world is sometimes an unfair place, and since you are very fortunate, you should try to remember those who do not share your good fortune. Try to give generously to those in need. It is likely that you will always have plenty, whereas many people have little, and no hope of change.

By learning to combine your good fortune with compassion, you should find that the quality of your life will be very high indeed.

YOUR CHINESE MONTH OF BIRTH

Find the table with your year of birth, and see where your birthday falls. For example, if you were born on August 30, 1957, you were born in Chinese month 8.

1 You are very skillful when dealing with difficult situations and make other people feel relaxed.

2 You dislike other people's advice and can be very harsh in your approach. Try to listen more.

3 You are kindhearted and assess situations well. Always try to keep your jealousy under control.

4 You are popular, an excellent organizer, and a good friend. You are also blessed with robust health.

5 You have enormous drive. You are very self-confident, but should also allow others to have their say.

6 You rarely give anything enough time or attention. Try to find a patient, helpful partner.

7 You are very efficient and a good judge of character, but be prepared to revise your opinions.

8 You are rather weak and upset people with your indifference. Try t[o] moderate your behavior.

9 You are a very charismatic individual and a natural performer. Your life may not always be easy.

10 You are popular, successful, and make an excellent leader. You suffer in silence from poor health.

11 You can be extremely naive, yet you still sail through life – much to other people's amazement.

12 Your emotions will lead you int[o] interesting situations, and your life should never be dull.

* Some Chinese years contain double months:	
1909: Month 2	1933: Month 5
Feb 22 – March 21	May 24 – June 22
March 22 – April 19	June 23 – July 21
1957: Month 8	1993: Month 3
Aug 25 – Sept 23	March 23 – April 2[1]
Sept 24 – Oct 22	April 22 – May 20

1909	
Jan 22 – Feb 21	1
See double months box	2
April 20 – May 18	3
May 19 – June 17	4
June 18 – July 16	5
July 17 – Aug 15	6
Aug 16 – Sept 13	7
Sept 14 – Oct 13	8
Oct 14 – Nov 12	9
Nov 13 – Dec 12	10
Dec 13 – Jan 10 1910	11
Jan 11 – Feb 9	12

1921	
Feb 8 – March 9	1
March 10 – April 7	2
April 8 – May 7	3
May 8 – June 5	4
June 6 – July 4	5
July 5 – Aug 3	6
Aug 4 – Sept 1	7
Sept 2 – Sept 30	8
Oct 1 – Oct 30	9
Oct 31 – Nov 28	10
Nov 29 – Dec 28	11
Dec 29 – Jan 27 1922	12

1933	
Jan 26 – Feb 23	1
Feb 24 – March 25	2
March 26 – April 24	3
April 25 – May 23	4
See double months box	5
July 22 – Aug 20	6
Aug 21 – Sept 19	7
Sept 20 – Oct 18	8
Oct 19 – Nov 17	9
Nov 18 – Dec 16	10
Dec 17 – Jan 14 1934	11
Jan 15 – Feb 13	12

1945	
Feb 13 – March 13	1
March 14 – April 11	2
April 12 – May 11	3
May 12 – June 9	4
June 10 – July 8	5
July 9 – Aug 7	6
Aug 8 – Sept 5	7
Sept 6 – Oct 5	8
Oct 6 – Nov 4	9
Nov 5 – Dec 4	10
Dec 5 – Jan 2 1946	11
Jan 3 – Feb 1	12

1957	
Jan 31 – March 1	1
March 2 – March 30	2
March 31 – April 29	3
April 30 – May 28	4
May 29 – June 27	5
June 28 – July 26	6
July 27 – Aug 24	7
See double months box	8
Oct 23 – Nov 21	9
Nov 22 – Dec 20	10
Dec 21 – Jan 19 1958	11
Jan 20 – Feb 17	12

1969	
Feb 17 – March 17	1
March 18 – April 16	2
April 17 – May 15	3
May 16 – June 14	4
June 15 – July 13	5
July 14 – Aug 12	6
Aug 13 – Sept 11	7
Sept 12 – Oct 10	8
Oct 11 – Nov 9	9
Nov 10 – Dec 8	10
Dec 9 – Jan 7 1970	11
Jan 8 – Feb 5	12

1981	
Feb 5 – March 5	1
March 6 – April 4	2
April 5 – May 3	3
May 4 – June 1	4
June 2 – July 1	5
July 2 – July 30	6
July 31 – Aug 28	7
Aug 29 – Sept 27	8
Sept 28 – Oct 27	9
Oct 28 – Nov 25	10
Nov 26 – Dec 25	11
Dec 26 – Jan 24 1982	12

1993	
Jan 23 – Feb 20	1
Feb 21 – March 22	2
See double months box	3
May 23 – June 19	4
June 20 – July 18	5
July 19 – Aug 17	6
Aug 18 – Sept 15	7
Sept 16 – Oct 14	8
Oct 15 – Nov 13	9
Nov 14 – Dec 12	10
Dec 13 – Jan 11 1994	11
Jan 12 – Feb 9	12

2005	
Feb 9 – March 9	1
March 10 – April 8	2
April 9 – May 7	3
May 8 – June 6	4
June 7 – July 5	5
July 6 – Aug 7	6
Aug 8 – Sept 3	7
Sept 4 – Oct 2	8
Oct 3 – Nov 1	9
Nov 2 – Nov 30	10
Dec 1 – Dec 30	11
Dec 31 – Jan 28 2006	12

YOUR CHINESE
DAY OF BIRTH

*Refer to the previous page to discover the beginning of your
Chinese month of birth, then use the chart below to
calculate your Chinese day of birth.*

If you were born on May 5, 1909,
your birthday is in the month starting
on April 20. Find 20 on the chart
below. Using 20 as the first day,
count the days until you reach the
date of your birthday. (Remember
that not all months contain 31 days.)
You were born on day 16 of the
Chinese month.

If you were born in a Chinese
double month, simply count the days
from the first date of the month that
contains your birthday.

1	2	3	4	5	6	7
8	9	10	11	12	13	14
15	16	17	18	19	20	21
22	23	24	25	26	27	28
29	30	31				

DAY 1, 10, 19, OR 28
You are trustworthy and set high
standards, but tend to rush your

projects. Try to be cautious, and do
not be too self-obsessed. You may
receive unexpected money but must
control your spending. You are
suited to a career in the public sector
or the arts.

DAY 2, 11, 20, OR 29
You are honest and popular. You
need peace, but also require lively
company. You are prone to
outbursts of temper. You tend to
enjoy life and make the most of your
opportunities. You are suited to a
literary or artistic career.

DAY 3, 12, 21, OR 30
You are quick-witted, but may
appear to be difficult. As a result,
people may be wary of being your
friend. You have a disciplined
character and fight for the truth. You
are suited to careers that have a
competitive element.

Day 4, 13, 22, or 31

You are very warmhearted, but also have a reserved attitude, which can sometimes make you appear unapproachable. If you try to be more outgoing and sociable, you should become more popular. You have a calm and patient manner, and are suited to a career as an academic or researcher.

Day 5, 14, or 23

Your fiery, obstinate nature can sometimes make it difficult for you to accept suggestions or opinions from others, and your stubbornness may lead to quarrels or problems. You should be lucky with money and may often use your profits to set up new projects. Your innate intelligence will enable you to cope with a demanding career.

Day 6, 15, or 24

You have an open, stable, and cheerful character, and enjoy an active social life. You are affectionate and emotional, and have a tendency to daydream. This can lead to confusion, and your eagerness to help others may be stifled by your indecision. Although you will never be wealthy, you should always have enough money.

Day 7, 16, or 25

You enjoy a certain amount of excitement in your life, but must learn to become more realistic and disciplined. Although you are a natural performer, you should beware of alienating your friends or colleagues. In your career, the opportunity to travel is more important to you than a good salary or a high standard of living.

Day 8, 17, or 26

You have very good judgment, but should not act too quickly. Your social skills may sometimes be lacking, and you may alienate other people, so try to be more tactful. You will experience poverty, but also wealth. Your calm and determined nature is combined with a free spirit, making you best suited to self-employment.

Day 9, 18, or 27

You are happy, optimistic, and warmhearted. You keep yourself busy and are rarely troubled by trivialities. Occasionally you quarrel unnecessarily with your friends, and it is important for you to learn to control your moods. You are particularly suited to a career as a sole owner or proprietor.

YOUR CHINESE HOUR OF BIRTH

In Chinese time, one hour is equal to two Western hours. Each Chinese double hour is associated with one of the twelve astrological animals.

11 P.M. – 1 A.M. RAT HOUR

You are independent and have a hot temper. Try to think before you speak. Your thrifty nature will be useful in business and at home. You are willing to help those who are close to you, and they will return your support.

1 – 3 A.M. OX HOUR

Up to the age of twenty, your life could be difficult, but your fortunes are likely to improve after these troublesome years. In your career, be prepared to take a risk or to leave home during your youth to achieve your goals. You should enjoy a prosperous old age.

3 – 5 A.M. TIGER HOUR

You have a lively and creative nature, which may cause family arguments in your youth. Between the ages of twenty and forty you may have many problems. Luckily, your fortunes are likely to improve dramatically in your forties.

5 – 7 A.M. RABBIT HOUR

Your parents should be helpful, but your siblings may be your rivals. You may have to move away from home to achieve your full potential at work. Your committed relationship may take time to become settled, but you should get along much better with everyone after middle age.

7 – 9 A.M. DRAGON HOUR

You have a quick-witted, determined, and attractive nature. Your life will be busy, but you could sometimes be lonely. You should achieve a good standard of living. Try to curb your excessive self-confidence, for it could make working relationships difficult.

9 – 11 A.M. SNAKE HOUR

You have a talent for business and should find it easy to build your career and provide for your family. You have a very generous spirit and will gladly help your friends when they are in trouble. Unfortunately, family relationships are unlikely to run smoothly.

11 A.M. – 1 P.M. HORSE HOUR

You are active, clever, and obstinate. Try to listen to advice. You are fascinated with travel and with changing your life. Learn to control your extravagance, for it could lead to financial suffering.

1 – 3 P.M. RAM HOUR

Steady relationships with your family, friends, or partners are difficult, because you have an active nature. You are clever, but must not force your views on others. Your fortunes will be at their lowest in your middle age.

3 – 5 P.M. MONKEY HOUR

You earn and spend money easily. Your character is attractive, but frustrating, too. Sometimes your parents are not able to give you adequate moral support. Your committed relationship should be good, but do not brood over emotional problems for too long – if you do your career could suffer.

5 – 7 P.M. ROOSTER HOUR

In your teenage years you may have many arguments with your family. There could even be a family division, which should eventually be resolved. You are trustworthy, kind, and warmhearted, and never intend to hurt other people.

7 – 9 P.M. DOG HOUR

Your brave, capable, hard-working nature is ideally suited to self-employment, and the forecast for your career is excellent. Try to control your impatience and vanity. The quality of your life is far more important to you than the amount of money you have saved.

9 – 11 P.M. PIG HOUR

You are particularly skilled at manual work and always set yourself high standards. Although you are warmhearted, you do not like to surround yourself with too many friends. However, the people who are close to you have your complete trust. You can be easily upset by others, but are able to forgive and forget quickly.

YOUR FORTUNE IN OTHER ANIMAL YEARS

The Rooster's fortunes fluctuate during the twelve animal years. It is best to concentrate on a year's positive aspects, and to take care when faced with the seemingly negative.

YEAR OF THE RAT
Your family life is highly auspicious in the Year of the Rat. A sense of happiness will be the common thread that links you with your relatives. There are likely to be many opportunities to celebrate the family's good fortune.

YEAR OF THE OX
You have the potential for success in the Year of the Ox. Unfortunately, there is a price to pay, in the form of hard work and struggle. Quarrels and disagreements could sap your energy; therefore, you should do your best to avoid them.

YEAR OF THE TIGER
This is an excellent year for your career, and you should make great progress. If you are self-employed, your business will flourish, and if you are an employee, you are likely to be promoted swiftly.

YEAR OF THE RABBIT
Financial success is likely to be yours in the Year of the Rabbit. However, you must make every effort to restrain your profligate streak. If you allow too much freedom, your financial rewards could diminish, or even disappear entirely.

YEAR OF THE DRAGON
This is potentially a very good year for the Rooster. The Year of the Dragon should bring you considerable success and happiness, and there is also a strong possibility that you could find yourself enjoying some fame and renown.

YEAR OF THE SNAKE
Your professional life is auspicious in the Year of the Snake, and you are likely to be promoted. However, be prepared for disappointment when your increased responsibilities do not necessarily correspond to increased financial rewards.

YEAR OF THE HORSE
It is important that you keep yourself under control in the Year of the Horse. It will be a demanding year in various areas of your life. However, do not give in to anger, frustration, or resentment, for you will only make matters worse.

YEAR OF THE RAM
In general, the Year of the Ram is a good year for the Rooster. However, in addition to enjoying a certain amount of success, you are also likely to find yourself responding to an underlying sadness or a sense of melancholy within your family.

YEAR OF THE MONKEY
At times, it may seem as if nothing is going right for you in the Year of the Monkey. Seemingly never-ending difficulties will depress and exhaust you, but try not to give in to despair, because this will invariably make matters worse.

YEAR OF THE ROOSTER
After the difficulties of last year, your own year can only be a marked improvement. Although you will be confronted by many problems throughout the year, you should be able to overcome them with ease.

YEAR OF THE DOG
Your fortune is mixed during the Year of the Dog. You should enjoy success at work and happiness in your family life. However, you may have to travel too often and too widely, and there could be difficulties ahead.

YEAR OF THE PIG
It is important that you take good care of yourself in the Year of the Pig, because you are particularly susceptible to ill health. Try to be cautious and vigilant, and watch out for potential accidents or troublesome incidents.

YOUR CHINESE
YEAR OF BIRTH

*Your astrological animal corresponds to the Chinese year of
your birth. It is the single most important key in the quest
to unlock your Chinese horoscope.*

Find your Western year of birth in
the left-hand column of the chart.
Your Chinese astrological animal is
on the same line as your year of birth
in the right-hand column of the
chart. If you were born in the
beginning of the year, check the

middle column of the chart carefully.
For example, if you were born in
1970, you might assume that you
belong to the Year of the Dog.
However, if your birthday falls
before February 6, you actually
belong to the Year of the Rooster.

1900	Jan 31 – Feb 18, 1901	Rat
1901	Feb 19 – Feb 7, 1902	Ox
1902	Feb 8 – Jan 28, 1903	Tiger
1903	Jan 29 – Feb 15, 1904	Rabbit
1904	Feb 16 – Feb 3, 1905	Dragon
1905	Feb 4 – Jan 24, 1906	Snake
1906	Jan 25 – Feb 12, 1907	Horse
1907	Feb 13 – Feb 1, 1908	Ram
1908	Feb 2 – Jan 21, 1909	Monkey
1909	Jan 22 – Feb 9, 1910	Rooster
1910	Feb 10 – Jan 29, 1911	Dog
1911	Jan 30 – Feb 17, 1912	Pig
1912	Feb 18 – Feb 5, 1913	Rat
1913	Feb 6 – Jan 25, 1914	Ox
1914	Jan 26 – Feb 13, 1915	Tiger
1915	Feb 14 – Feb 2, 1916	Rabbit
1916	Feb 3 – Jan 22, 1917	Dragon

1917	Jan 23 – Feb 10, 1918	Snake
1918	Feb 11 – Jan 31, 1919	Horse
1919	Feb 1 – Feb 19, 1920	Ram
1920	Feb 20 – Feb 7, 1921	Monkey
1921	Feb 8 – Jan 27, 1922	Rooster
1922	Jan 28 – Feb 15, 1923	Dog
1923	Feb 16 – Feb 4, 1924	Pig
1924	Feb 5 – Jan 23, 1925	Rat
1925	Jan 24 – Feb 12, 1926	Ox
1926	Feb 13 – Feb 1, 1927	Tiger
1927	Feb 2 – Jan 22, 1928	Rabbit
1928	Jan 23 – Feb 9, 1929	Dragon
1929	Feb 10 – Jan 29, 1930	Snake
1930	Jan 30 – Feb 16, 1931	Horse
1931	Feb 17 – Feb 5, 1932	Ram
1932	Feb 6 – Jan 25, 1933	Monkey
1933	Jan 26 – Feb 13, 1934	Rooster

1934	Feb 14 – Feb 3, 1935	Dog		1971	Jan 27 – Feb 14, 1972	Pig
1935	Feb 4 – Jan 23, 1936	Pig		1972	Feb 15 – Feb 2, 1973	Rat
1936	Jan 24 – Feb 10, 1937	Rat		1973	Feb 3 – Jan 22, 1974	Ox
1937	Feb 11 – Jan 30, 1938	Ox		1974	Jan 23 – Feb 10, 1975	Tiger
1938	Jan 31 – Feb 18, 1939	Tiger		1975	Feb 11 – Jan 30, 1976	Rabbit
1939	Feb 19 – Feb 7, 1940	Rabbit		1976	Jan 31 – Feb 17, 1977	Dragon
1940	Feb 8 – Jan 26, 1941	Dragon		1977	Feb 18 – Feb 6, 1978	Snake
1941	Jan 27 – Feb 14, 1942	Snake		1978	Feb 7 – Jan 27, 1979	Horse
1942	Feb 15 – Feb 4, 1943	Horse		1979	Jan 28 – Feb 15, 1980	Ram
1943	Feb 5 – Jan 24, 1944	Ram		1980	Feb 16 – Feb 4, 1981	Monkey
1944	Jan 25 – Feb 12, 1945	Monkey		1981	Feb 5 – Jan 24, 1982	Rooster
1945	Feb 13 – Feb 1, 1946	Rooster		1982	Jan 25 – Feb 12, 1983	Dog
1946	Feb 2 – Jan 21, 1947	Dog		1983	Feb 13 – Feb 1, 1984	Pig
1947	Jan 22 – Feb 9, 1948	Pig		1984	Feb 2 – Feb 19, 1985	Rat
1948	Feb 10 – Jan 28, 1949	Rat		1985	Feb 20 – Feb 8, 1986	Ox
1949	Jan 29 – Feb 16, 1950	Ox		1986	Feb 9 – Jan 28, 1987	Tiger
1950	Feb 17 – Feb 5, 1951	Tiger		1987	Jan 29 – Feb 16, 1988	Rabbit
1951	Feb 6 – Jan 26, 1952	Rabbit		1988	Feb 17 – Feb 5, 1989	Dragon
1952	Jan 27 – Feb 13, 1953	Dragon		1989	Feb 6 – Jan 26, 1990	Snake
1953	Feb 14 – Feb 2, 1954	Snake		1990	Jan 27 – Feb 14, 1991	Horse
1954	Feb 3 – Jan 23, 1955	Horse		1991	Feb 15 – Feb 3, 1992	Ram
1955	Jan 24 – Feb 11, 1956	Ram		1992	Feb 4 – Jan 22, 1993	Monkey
1956	Feb 12 – Jan 30, 1957	Monkey		1993	Jan 23 – Feb 9, 1994	Rooster
1957	Jan 31 – Feb 17, 1958	Rooster		1994	Feb 10 – Jan 30, 1995	Dog
1958	Feb 18 – Feb 7, 1959	Dog		1995	Jan 31 – Feb 18, 1996	Pig
1959	Feb 8 – Jan 27, 1960	Pig		1996	Feb 19 – Feb 6, 1997	Rat
1960	Jan 28 – Feb 14, 1961	Rat		1997	Feb 7 – Jan 27, 1998	Ox
1961	Feb 15 – Feb 4, 1962	Ox		1998	Jan 28 – Feb 15, 1999	Tiger
1962	Feb 5 – Jan 24, 1963	Tiger		1999	Feb 16 – Feb 4, 2000	Rabbit
1963	Jan 25 – Feb 12, 1964	Rabbit		2000	Feb 5 – Jan 23, 2001	Dragon
1964	Feb 13 – Feb 1, 1965	Dragon		2001	Jan 24 – Feb 11, 2002	Snake
1965	Feb 2 – Jan 20, 1966	Snake		2002	Feb 12 – Jan 31, 2003	Horse
1966	Jan 21 – Feb 8, 1967	Horse		2003	Feb 1 – Jan 21, 2004	Ram
1967	Feb 9 – Jan 29, 1968	Ram		2004	Jan 22 – Feb 8, 2005	Monkey
1968	Jan 30 – Feb 16, 1969	Monkey		2005	Feb 9 – Jan 28, 2006	Rooster
1969	Feb 17 – Feb 5, 1970	Rooster		2006	Jan 29 – Feb 17, 2007	Dog
1970	Feb 6 – Jan 26, 1971	Dog		2007	Feb 18 – Feb 6, 2008	Pig